FRE

Speak French Now!

A beginner guide to instantly start speaking French.

(without sounding like an idiot)

FOREIGN LANGUAGE GUIDES

Copyright © 2014 BeautyBodyStyle, LLC
All rights reserved. No part of this book may be reproduced in any form or by any electronic or mechanical means including information storage and retrieval systems – except in the case of brief quotations in articles or reviews – without the permission in writing from its publisher.

Although the author and publisher have made every effort to ensure that the information in this book was correct at press time, the author and publisher do not assume and hereby disclaim any liability to any party for any loss, damage, or disruption caused by errors or omissions, whether such errors or omissions result from negligence, accident, or any other cause.

Cover image: France Grunge Flags
Image use under CC-BY License

ISBN: 1515376427
ISBN-13: 978-1515376422

"The limits of my language means the limits of my world." - Ludwig Wittgenstein

CONTENTS

	Introduction	8
1	Essential Basic Phrases	9
2	French Pronunciation	16
3	The Alphabet	23
4	Nouns, Articles and Demonstratives	25
5	Good Words to Know	28
6	Subject Pronouns	31
7	To Be and to Have	33
8	Asking Questions	37
9	Numbers	39
10	Days of the Week	42
11	Months of the Year	44
12	Seasons	46
13	Directions	47
14	Color and Shapes	49
15	Weather	52
16	Time	54
17	Family and Animals	56

18	To Know	60
19	Formation of Plural Noun	62
20	Possessive Adjectives	64
21	To Do or Make	67
22	School & Jobs	69
23	Prepositions and Contractions	76
24	Conjugating Regular Verbs	80
25	To Take, Eat or Drink	86
26	Food and Meals	88
27	Fruits, Vegetables, Meats	91
28	Quantities	95
29	Irregularities in Regular Verbs	97
30	Past Indefinite Tense	101
31	Irregular Past Participles	103
32	Etre Verbs	105
33	Holiday Phrases	108

INTRODUCTION

You have decided to learn French?

Congratulations!

You are about to enter an amazing, romantic, fascinating, historic and artful world like no other! The French language has been made easy to learn with this course and gaining some insight into both the language and the country will certainly pay off, as France is truly exceptional.

The country, which shares borders with Belgium, Germany, Switzerland, Spain, Monaco, Andorra and Luxemburg, has a population of 63.4 million people. Most of them live in big cities, such as Paris, Marseille, Lyon and Toulouse. France is where you can find world-famous works of art, such as the Mona Lisa painting by Leonardo da Vinci and enjoy the most extraordinary fashion, especially in Paris where people are well-known for their distinguished style.

France's nature combines the thrills of ski slopes in the Alps and beach adventures on the French Riviera. But the country is perhaps best known for its culinary achievements and wine industry – a combination that is known to form true magic!

Get started on your French learning experience and uncover the most fascinating French facts with this vocabulary and grammar packed learning program!

1 ESSENTIAL BASIC PHRASES

Imagine you have won a trip to France and are now roaming the picturesque, iconic streets of Paris. Everyone around is dressed in sharp yet really creative clothing, the famous street cafes are bustling with vibrant people of all ages, the sun is shining and you are on your way to see some of the most popular attractions in the world. Perhaps you will even do a little shopping down luxurious Champs Elysees; you are in France after all. This dreamy scenario can quickly turn into a real nightmare if you are unable to exchange two sentences with anyone. But don't worry – you don't actually need to learn the entire language to warm the French hearts and immerse yourself in this unique culture. The best way to start is by learning some basic phrases, such as greetings and expressions. Even if you get them wrong at first (you are human like the rest of us), soon you will realize how fun it is to speak French, even with the basics!

Bonjour *(bohn-zhoor)*

Hello / Good day

Bonsoir / Bonne nuit

(bohn-swahr/bun nwee)

Good evening / Good night (only said when going to bed)

Au revoir!

(ohr-vwah)

Goodbye!

Merci beaucoup

(mair-see boh-koo)

Thank you very much

S'il vous plaît

(seel voo pleh)

Please

Je vous en prie / de rien)

(zhuh voo zawn pree/duh ree-ahn)

You're welcome.

Oui / non

(wee/nohn)

Yes / no

Monsieur, Madame, Mademoiselle

(muh-syuh, mah-dahm, mahd-mwah-zell)

Mister, Misses, Miss

Ça va?

(sah vah)

How are you? (informal)

Comment allez-vous?

(koh-mawn tahl-ay voo)

How are you? (formal)

Je vais bien

(zhuh vay bee-ahn)

I'm fine

Ça va bien / mal / pas mal

(sah vah bee-ahn/mahl/pah mahl)

I'm good / bad / not bad

Je suis fatigué(e)

(zhuh swee fah-tee-gay)

I'm tired

J'ai faim

(zhay fawn)

I'm hungry

J'ai soif

(zhay swahf)

I'm thirsty

Je suis malade

(zhuh swee mah-lahd)

I'm sick

Comment vous appelez-vous?

(koh-mawn voo zah-play voo)

What's your name? (formal)

Comment t'appelles-tu?

(koh-mawn tah-pell tew)

What's your name? (informal)

Je m'appelle...

(zhuh mah-pell)

I am called...

Mon nom est...

(mohn nohm ay)

My name is...

Vous êtes d'où?

(voo zet doo)

Where are you from? (formal)

Tu es d'où?

(tew ay doo)

Where are you from? (informal)

Où habitez-vous?

(ooh ah-bee-tay voo)

Where do you live? (formal)

Où habites-tu?

(ooh ah-beet tew)

Where do you live? (informal)

Je suis des Etats-Unis / du Canada.

(zhuh swee day zay-tahz-ew-nee/dew kah-nah-dah)

I am from the United States / Canada.

J'habite aux Etats-Unis / au Canada.

(zhah-beet oh zay-tahz-ew-nee/ oh kah-nah-dah)

I live in the U.S. / Canada.

Vous avez quel âge?

(voo za-vay kell ahzh)

How old are you? (formal)

Tu as quel âge?

(tew ah kell ahzh)

How old are you? (informal)

J'ai _____ ans.

(zhay _____ awn)

I am _____ years old.

Parlez-vous français?

(par-lay voo frahn-say)

Do you speak French? (formal)

Parles-tu anglais?

(parl tew on-glay)

Do you speak English? (informal)

Italien, Allemand, Espagnol

(ee-tahl-ee-ahn, ahll-uh-mawn, es-pahn-yol)

Italian, German, Spanish

Russe, Japonais, Chinois

(rooss, zhah-po-neh, shee-nwah)

Russian, Japanese, Chinese

Je parle…

(zhuh parl)

I speak…

Je ne parle pas…

(zhuh nuh parl pah)

I don't speak…

Je (ne) comprends (pas)

(zhuh nuh com-prawn pah)

I (don't) understand

Je (ne) sais (pas)

(zhuhn say pah)

I (don't) know

Excusez-moi / Pardonnez-moi

(eg-scew-zay mwah/par-dohn-ay mwah)

Excuse me / Pardon me

Je regrette / Je suis désolé(e)

(zhuh re-gret/zhuh swee day-zoh-lay)

I'm sorry

A tout à l'heure / A bientôt

(ah too tah luhr/ah bee-ahn-toh)

See you later / See you soon

Salut

(sah-lew)

Hi / Bye

Je t'aime

(zhuh tem)

I love you (singular)

Je vous aime

(zhuh voo zem)

I love you! (plural)

2 FRENCH PRONUNCIATION

The French have one unmistakable trait – their unique pronunciation, especially in the face of the unmistakable "r". The way they twist and swirl the words around sounds almost like music, no wonder it is said to be the most romantic language in the world! But knowing the words alone is not enough to produce this melodic rhythm – you need the right pronunciation. French articulation might be a little tricky for English speakers to master at first, but soon you will find that you have gained full control over this unique ability. Don't worry too much about the way you sound – just relax and let French pronunciation take over! After all, being a real French is all about effortless elegance and one way to mimic it is by using your pronunciation.

French letter(s)

a, à, â

Sounds like: ah

é, et, and final er and ez

Sounds like: ay

e, è, ê, ai, ei, ais

Sounds like: eh

i, y

Sounds like: ee

o

Sounds like: oh

ou

Sounds like: oo

oy, oi

Sounds like: wah

u

Sounds like: ew

u + vowel

Sounds like: wee

c (before e, i, y)

Sounds like: s

s

Sounds like: s

ç (before a, o, u)

Sounds like: s

c (before a, o, u)

Sounds like: k

g (before e, i, y)

Sounds like: zh

ge (before a, o)

Sounds like: zh

g (before a, o, u)

Sounds like: g

gn

Sounds like: nyuh

h

Sounds like: nothing, it is silent.

j

Sounds like: zh

qu, final q

Sounds like: k

r

Sounds like: a rolled r

s (between vowels)

Sounds like: z

Th

Sounds like: t

x

Sounds like: ekss. The exceptions are six & dix

where it sounds like an s and soixante where it sounds like a z.

Pronouncing French correctly can be a little tricky for beginners due to the amount of silent letters. A rule of thumb to note is that if a word ends in C, F, L or R you will typically pronounce the final consonant. The exception to this with respect to R, are verbs that in r. In this instance the R will remain silent.

A key thing to note when learning French pronunciation is that the French slur many of their words together and this is commonly referred to as liaison.

For example, if a word ends with a consonant that is not pronounced and the next word begins with a vowel or silent h, you will slur the two together as if it were one word.

Here are a list of indicators of where the liaison will be used:

• after a determiner (words like *un, des, les, mon, ces, quels*)

• before or after a pronoun (*vous avez, je les ai*)

• after a preceding adjective (*bon ami, petits enfants*)

• after one syllable prepositions (*en avion, dans un livre*)

- after some one syllable adverbs (*très, plus, bien*)
- after *est*

It is sometimes used after *pas, trop fort*, and the forms of *être*, but it is never made after *et*.

You will also find that the *e* is sometimes dropped in words and phrases, which also causes a slur in the pronunciation.

For example:

- rapid(e)ment, (pronounced *ra-peed-mawn*, not *ra-peed-uh-mawn*)

- sous l(e) bureau (pronounced *sool bewr-oh*, not *soo luh bewr-oh*)

- il a d(e) bons copains (*eel ahd bohn ko-pahn*, not *eel ah duh bohn ko-pahn*)

- il y a d(e)... , pas d(e)... , plus d(e)... (*eel yahd, pahd, plewd*, not *eel ee ah duh, pah duh,* or *plew duh*)

- je n(e), de n(e) (*zhuhn, duhn,* not *zhuh nuh* or *duh nuh*)

In general, intonation only rises for yes/no questions, and all other times, it goes down at the end of the sentence.

Two sounds that are tricky to an American English speaker are the differences between the long and short u and e. The long u (ou) is pronounced oooh, as in hoot. The short u (u) does not exist in English though. To pronounce is correctly, round your lips as if to whistle, and then say eee.

The long (è) and short e (é) are relatively easy to pronounce, but sometimes it is difficult to hear the difference. The long e is pronounced openly, like ay, as in play. The short e is more closed, and pronounced like eh, as in bed.

And of course, the French R. This is what presents the most problems for English speakers. In English, when we pronounce r, we use the front of our tongue and not the back like the French do. For example, say "read". Did you notice how when you pronounce the r, the tip of your tongue goes up?

In order to achieve the correct pronunciation of the French R, place the tip of your tongue against the bottom row of your teeth and keep it there when pronouncing r. By keeping the tip of your tongue down, you force the back of your tongue in the correct position to make the French r sound.

Try it.

Sounds funny, huh?

Okay, it's going to take practice but before long you will master the correct pronunciation of the French R.

3 THE ALPHABET

You might not want to craft complicated novels in French, such as one of the most famous French authors – Victor Hugo, not just yet anyway, but you still need to get acquainted with the alphabet. How else would you read the signs to Avenue Montaigne, Rue de Rivoli and other fascinating corners of France?

More importantly, how would you manage to choose your favorite dishes within the menus of elegant Parisian restaurants? Even if you have been seated at a place offering the best of famous French wines, no one wants to order a drink that they cannot read the name of. The alphabet may seem like a small step into the language, but it is actually your essential key to French – the only way you can get the most out of both the country and language.

a (ah)

b (beh)

c (seh)

d (deh)

e (uh)

f (eff)

g (zheh)

h (ahsh)

i (ee)

FOREIGN LANGUAGE GUIDES

j (zhee)

k (kah)

l (ell)

m (em)

n (en)

o (oh)

p (peh)

q (koo)

r (air)

s (ess)

t (teh)

u (ooh)

v (veh)

w (doo-blah-veh)

x (eeks)

y (ee-grek)

z (zed)

4 NOUNS, ARTICLES AND DEMONSTRATIVES

Have you lived your entire life believing that a table is an "it"? If the answer is yes, you may be surprised to learn that the French don't see it that way. Every noun in the French language can have a different "gender", which is indicated by different articles. You would have never thought how much fun it would be to give all the humdrum objects of your everyday life an actual gender and you will almost certainly be entertained by the French ways. Want to point to something specific, perhaps a nice Chanel bag, then you would need your demonstratives. By learning the correct ways to use nouns, articles and demonstratives in French, you will take a very confident step into learning to speak just like a native!

All nouns in French have a gender, either masculine or feminine. Generally speaking, you will need to memorize the gender as you learn, but there are some indicators that will help you determine which gender a noun is.

For example,

Nouns ending in -age and -ment are usually masculine, as are nouns ending with a consonant.

Nouns ending in -ure, -sion, -tion, -ence, -ance, -té, and -ette are usually feminine.

When speaking French both the articles and adjectives need to agree in number and ender with the nouns they modify. Articles and adjectives must agree in number and gender with the nouns they modify.

Definite Articles (The)

Masculine

Le lit. The bed.

Feminine

La pomme. The apple.

Before a vowel

L'oiseau. The bird.

Plural

Les gants. The gloves.

Indefinite Articles (A, An, Some)

Masculine

Un lit. A bed.

Feminine

Une pomme. An apple

Plural

Des gants. Some gloves

Demonstrative Adjectives (This, That, These, Those)

Masculine

ce lit this/that bed

Masculine, Before Vowel

cet oiseau this/that bird

Feminine

cette pomme this/that apple

Plural

ces gants these/those gloves

If you need to make a distinction between this or that and these or those, you can simply add -ci to the end of the noun for this and these, and -là to the end of the noun for that and those.

For example, ce lit-ci is this bed, while ce lit-là is that bed.

5 GOOD WORDS TO KNOW AND COMMON VOCABULARY

Have you ever gone to a foreign country and tried to use a phrasebook? Ordering a full cream Macchiato or trying to ask a local about the most authentic parts of the city may be a struggle when you are flipping through the phrasebook pages. Even if you are a real trooper and manage the task, when you actually get an answer in native speed the phrasebook will find itself out of depth.

That is why it is really important to learn some useful words and general vocabulary in French. You may not have mastered the entire language just yet, but kicking the phrasebook to the curb because you can manage on your own, is immensely satisfactory! Try some of the new words you have learned on your friends and you will definitely have an impressed audience.

What is more, if you have plans of visiting France or doing business with French partners, being able to say at least a few words in their native language will certainly pave the way to a good conversation. People in France tend to really appreciate any effort being made by a foreigner to speak French.

c'est (say) It's / That's

il y a (eel-ee-yah) There is/are

voilà (vwah-lah) There is/are

voice (vwah-see) Here is/are

et (ay) and

toujours (too-zhoor) always

mais (may) but

souvent (soo-vawn) often

maintenant (mahnt-nawn) now

quelquefois (kell-kuh-fwah) sometimes

surtout (sir-too) especially

d'habitude (dah-bee-tewd) usually

sauf (sohf) except

aussi (oh-see) also, too

bien sûr (bee-ahn sir) of course

encore (awn-kore) again

comme ci, comme ça (kohm see kohm sah) so so

en retard (awn-ruh-tar) late

pas mal (pah mal) not bad

presque (presk) almost

le livre (leevr) book

une amie (ew nah-mee) friend (fem)

un ami (ah-nah-mee) friend (masc)

le crayon (krah-yohn) pencil

le stylo (stee-loh) Pen

le papier pah-pyaya paper

une femme (ewn fawn) woman

un home (ah-nohm) Man

un garcon (gar-sohn) Boy

une fille (feey) girl

le chien (shee-ahn) dog

le chat (shah) cat

6 SUBJECT PRONOUNS

Have you encountered a poorly written article or book where the names of the protagonists keep being mentioned? You have probably found that it is quite tedious to read and sounds completely amateur – something that the French are definitely not. The French language is delicate and refined so to keep repeating names, or subjects, will tear you away from its beauty. That is why you need subject pronouns. Don't worry though, they are fairly simple to learn and can make all the difference in building your mastery of the language. Imagine taking a boat ride down beautiful river Seine and having the satisfaction of saying to your French companions "Look – they are waving to us from ashore!"

French Subject Pronouns

Je (zhuh) = I

Tu (tew) = You (informal)

Il (eel) = He

Elle (ell) = She

On (ohn) = One

Nous (noo) = We

Vous (voo) = You (formal and plural)

Ils (eel) = They (masculine)

Elles (ell) = They (feminine)

Il, ils and elle, elles can also mean it when they replace a noun (il/ils replaces masculine nouns, and elle/elles replaces feminine nouns) instead of a person's name.

In French, there are two ways to say you.

Tu (informal) is used when speaking to children, animals, or close friends and family.

Vous (formal) is used when speaking to more than one person, or to someone you don't know or who is older. On can be translated into English as one, the people, we, they, or you.

7 TO BE AND TO HAVE

To be a French speaker means making an art out of lunch, loving raspberries, having long picnics, kissing on the cheek and a ton of other charismatic characteristics. As a French, it is important to have impeccable taste, an eye for the beauty in the world, appreciation for great parties and heaps of other fantastic qualities. To be and to have are vital for describing the enchanting way of French living and so you simply cannot leave them out of your vocabulary. These are two of the most essential verbs for making sentences. Combine them with the key vocabulary you already know and it you might be able to keep an entire conversation going!

Present tense of être (eh-truh) - to be

Je suis (zhuh swee) I am

Tu es (tew ay) You are

Vous êtes (voo zett) You are

Nous sommes (noo sohm) We are

Il est (eel ay) He is

Elle est (ell ay) She is

On est (ohn ay) One is

Ils sont (eel sohn) They are

Elles sont (ell sohn) They are

Common French expressions that use être:

être de retour - to be back

être en retard - to be late

être en avance - to be early

être d'accord - to be in agreement

être sur le point de - to be about to

être en train de - to be in the act of

être enrhumée - to have a cold

nous + être (un jour) - to be (a day)

How to Say It:

Je suis en retard! *I'm late!*

Tu es en avance. *You are early.*

Elle est d'accord. *She agrees.*

Nous sommes lundi. *It is Monday.*

Vous êtes enrhumé. *You have a cold.*

Ils sont en train d'étudier. *They are studying.*

Elles sont sur le point de partir. *They are about to leave.*

On est de retour. *The people are back.*

Present tense of avoir - to have (ah-vwahr):

j'ai (zhay) I have

as (ah) You have

avez (ah-vay) You have

a (ah) He/she has

avons (ah-vohn) We have

ont (ohn) They have

Common French expressions that use avoir:

avoir chaud - to be hot

avoir froid - to be cold

avoir peur - to be afraid

avoir raison - to be right

avoir tort - to be wrong

avoir faim - to be hungry

avoir soif - to be thirsty

avoir sommeil - to be sleepy

avoir honte - to be ashamed

avoir besoin de - to need

avoir l'air de - to look like, seem

avoir envie de - to feel like

avoir de la chance - to be lucky

How to Say It:

J'ai froid. *I'm cold.*

Tu as raison. *You are right.*

Il a sommeil ce soir. *He is tired tonight.*

Elle a de la chance! *She's lucky!*

Nous avons faim. *We are hungry.*

Vouz avez tort. *You are wrong.*

Ils ont chaud. *They are hot.*

Elles ont peur. *They are afraid.*

8 ASKING QUESTIONS

Have you ever been to France? Do you enjoy aromatic wines? What do you think about the French dessert soufflé? How was the view from the Eifel Tower? Healthy curiosity, or interested enthusiasm, is characteristic of France and for a good reason – there is so much to learn about this country with rich history and culture that you simply cannot help but ask heaps of questions.

However, how would you be able to get the most interesting French secrets out if you don't know how to form your questions? French mysteries spread beyond famous literary works such as "Le parfum de la dame en noir" or "Murder in Belleville". Sights such as the cathedral Notre Dame de Paris hold many of their own precious secrets and the way to uncover them is through asking questions. Forming a questions is much like learning a mathematical formula – once you get the hang of it is really easy to do. So get started with your questions to satisfy that French curiosity!

French Question Words

Qui (kee) = Who

Qui êtes-vous? Who are you?

Quoi (kwah) = What

Quoi de neuf? What's new?

Pourquoi (poor-kwah) = Why

Pourquoi pas? Why not?

Quand (kawn) = When

Quand arrive le train à Paris? When does the train arrive in Paris?

Où (ooh) = Where

Où est la salle de bain? Where is the bathroom?

Comment (kohn-mawn) = How

Comment dites-vous? How do you say?

Combien (kohn-bee-ahn) = How much / many

Combien de fois avez-vous été ici? How many times have you been here?

Quel(le) (kehl) = Which / what

Quelle heure est-il? What time is it?

9 NUMBERS

Did you know that around 10 million Americans speak French, while about 35% of the French speak English; the number of times people kiss each other on the cheek in France depends on the region but can be up to 5; you can find over 400 varieties of French cheese; each year 75 million tourists visit France; 20% of the French people live in the regions around Paris; France is second in the world for film production.

Numbers and ordinals can tell you a lot about the place and help you learn some pretty fascinating facts. Naturally, not being able to use numbers means staying forever away from all the exciting details of France and the French people, which you could otherwise learn. And besides not knowing the numbers in French means not being able to shop any Parisian couture or write down the phone number of an interesting French person you met!

0 Zéro (zay-roh)

1 Un (ahn) One

2 Deux (duh)

3 Trois (twah)

4 Quatre (kat)

5 Cinq (sahn)

6 Six (sees)

7 Sept (set)

8 Huit (weet)

9 Neuf (nuhf)

10 Dix (deess)

11 Onze (ohnz)

12 Douze (dooz)

13 Treize (trehz)

14 Quatorze (kah-tohrz)

15 Quinze (kanz)

16 Seize (sez)

17 Dix-sept (dee-set)

18 Dix-huit (deez-weet)

19 Dix-neuf (deez-nuhf)

20 Vingt (vahn)

21 Vingt et un (vahn tay ahn)

22 Vingt-deux (vahn duh)

23 Vingt-trois (vahn twah)

30 Trente (trawnt)

31 Trente et un (trawnt ay uhn)

32 Trente-deux (trawnt duh)

40 Quarante (kuh-rawnt)

50 Cinquante (sank-awnt)

60 Soixante (swah-ssawnt)

70 Soixante-diz (swah-ssawnt deez)

71 Soixante et onze (swah-ssawnt ay ohnz)

72 Soixante-douze (swah-ssawnt dooz)

80 Quatre-vingts (ka-truh vahn)

81 Quatre-vingt-un (ka-truh vahn than)

82 Quatre-vingt-deux (ka-truh vahn duh)

90 Quatre-vingt-dix (ka-truh vahn deez)

91 Quatre-vingt-onze (ka-truh vahn ohnz)

92 Quatre-vingt-douze (ka-truh vahn dooz)

100 Cent (sawnt)

101 Cent un (sawnt ahn)

200 Deux cents (duh sawnt)

201 Deux cent un (duh sawnt ahn)

1,000 Mille (meel)

2,000 Deux mille (duh meel)

1,000,000 Un million (ahn meel-ee-ohn)

10 DAYS OF THE WEEK

As unbelievable as it may sound, around 2 new cookbooks are published every day in France – that is how much the French appreciate truly good food. And, of course every day of the week has to be greeted with a new, more delicious meal. Besides, every day of the week in France, especially in Large cities such as Paris, Nantes and Lyon there is a different cultural event worth visiting. Imagine walking by an advertisement for the gallery opening of the month or the most awaited new gourmet restaurant, and not knowing when to go simply because you don't understand the days of the week! After all, they are only 7 so not knowing them is really not worth it.

Lundi (lahn-dee) Monday

Mardi (mahr-dee) Tuesday

Mercredi (mare-kruh-dee) Wednesday

Jeudi (zhuh-dee) Thursday

Vendredi (vahn-druh-dee) Friday

Samedi (sahm-dee) Saturday

Dimanche (dee-mahnsh) Sunday

le jour (luh zhoor) day

la semaine (lah suh-men) week

aujourd'hui (oh-zhoor-dwee) today

hier (ee-air) yesterday

demain (duh-mahn) tomorrow

CHAPTER 11: MONTHS OF THE YEAR

Paris is amazing in April – the trees down Promenade Plantee, or tree-lined walkways, are just beginning to bloom and you can sense their pleasant aroma for miles. If you find yourself along the Parisian streets in July, it can be a bit hot, but there is a great advantage – the Parc de la Villette, where you can attend film festivals held on lush green lawns. And what about some January skiing and snowboarding down the world-famous, breathtaking slopes of the French Alps? Every month has something special and spectacular to offer but to take advantage, you first need to know the months of the year in French. Every region of France is most appealing during a different period and you can only ever fully appreciate the experience if you know the best month for a visit.

Janvier (zhan-vee-ay) January

Février (fay-vree-ay) February

Mars (marz) March

Avril (ah-vril) April

Mai (may-ee) May

Juin (zhwahn) June

Juillet (zhwee-ay) July

Août (oot) August

Septembre (sep-tawm-bruh) September

Octobre (ahk-toh-bruh) October

Novembre (noh-vawm-bruh) November

Décembre (day-sawm-bruh) December

le mois (luh mwah) Month

l'an / l'année (lawn/law-nay) Year

12 SEASONS

Can you imagine spending your next summer in the South of France? Touring the beaches of Cannes and St. Tropez, tasting the delicate wines of Nice and Marseille...A summer in France can turn into an unforgettable holiday that many dream of. What about spending your spring break in Paris? You could marvel at the Eifel tower through the blooming flower beds along the streets. Spend entire days in the green paradise of Parc des Buttes-Chaumont, reading a great book or maybe even your guide to the French capital. A fall trip to France can be a real once in a lifetime experience for food enthusiasts – this is when you can see wild mushrooms being picked and when the olive and fig harvest are richest. Winter in France, on the other hand, is uniquely romantic and offers great ski resorts that you can enjoy even if you don't practice any extreme sports. But for you to get a taste of all of that greatness, you first need to learn the seasons in French.

l'été (lay-tay) Summer

en été (awn ay-tay) in the summer

l'automne (loh-tohn) Fall

en automne (aw noh-tohn) in the fall

l'hiver (lee-vair) Winter

en hiver (aw nee-vair) in the winter

le printemps (luh prahn-tawn) Spring

au printemps (oh prahn-tawn) in the spring

13 DIRECTIONS

Imagine sitting on a beautifully crafted bench in Toulouse and wanting to reach the magnificent Toulouse Cathedral, the impressive Capitole de Toulouse or the peaceful confound of Chateau de Pibrac. Waving the map around, turning it side to side and trying to figure out which way to go can only ruin your trip to this fascinating city. Of course you would be spared the hassle if only you could ask for directions. Being able to ask a passer-by how to reach your next destination and recognizing the difference between left and right in French are your first key tasks to mastering French orientation. You will definitely have plenty of use for this lesson!

le nord (luh nor) North

le sud (luh sewd) South

l'est (lest) East

l'ouest (lwest) West

La carte (lah cart) The map

Rue (roo) Street

Où est...? (ooo eh) Where is...?

Comment est-ce que je vais à ... ? (commaw es kuh zhuh vay za...) How do I get to...?

C'est loin? (say lawn) Is it far?

À droite (ah drwat) Right

FOREIGN LANGUAGE GUIDES

À gauche (ah goh-sh) Left

Tout droit (too drwah) Straight

Devant (duh-vahn) In front of

14 COLOR AND SHAPES

The French love their country, rightfully so if we may add, and have a great appreciation for everyone who is just as excited about France. But imagine you had to describe the French flag to anyone, or the intricate shapes of the Triumphal arch in Paris – would you be able to do it without knowing the words for colors and shapes? Besides, if you want to blend in with the locals, instead of stand out like a tourist, on your next visit to the country you need to be up to code with all the latest trends of artistic French fashion. Your key to French style is learning the words for shapes and colors, thus being able to absorb all the trending cuts and hues with ease. France is a country of diversity and art, which you will be able to view differently after learning about shapes and colors.

In French, adjectives also have a gender.

An example of this is vert/e (green).

Vert is the masculine form of green and *verte* is the feminine form.

With French you will find that almost all adjectives agree in gender and number with the noun they modify (the exception is marron and orange, as well as colors that are modified with the words clair-light and foncé-dark). Additionally, most adjectives are placed after the noun.

For example, *un carré brun* is a brown square and *une boîte noire* is a black box.

rouge (roozh) Red

orange (oh-rahnzh) Orange

jaune (zhohn) Yellow

vert/e (vehr/t) Green

bleu/e (bluh) Blue

pourpre, violet/te (poo-pruh, vee-oh-leh/let) Purple

blanc/he (blawn/sh) White

brun/e, marron (brahn/brewn, mah-rohn) Brown

noir/e (nwahr) Black

rose (roze) Pink

doré/e (doh-ray) Gold

argenté/e (ahr-zhawn-tay) Silver

gris/e (gree/z) Gray

le carré (kah-ray) square

le cercle (sair-kluh) circle

le triangle (tree-awn-gluh) triangle

l'octogone (ok-toh-gohn) octagon

une boîte (bwaht) box

le cône (kohn) cone

le cylinder (see-lahn-druh) cylinder

la sphere (sfair) sphere

le cube (kewb) cube

le rectangle (ruhk-tawn-gluh) rectangle

l'ovale (loh-vahl) oval

15 WEATHER

Even though there are countries much bigger than beautiful France, the climate in this region is extremely versatile, giving you the opportunity to encounter all sorts of weather. Of course, every region and activity in France is best experienced during various weather conditions and so your best option is to learn all the weather and climate descriptions, so next time you want to climb on top of the Eifel Tower your can actually marvel at the view, instead of being restrained by the fog and rain. France is divided into four distinct climate areas and before you can have the trip of your life you need to be able to understand the weather forecast for all of them.

Quel temps fait-il? (kell tawn fay-teel) What's the weather like?

Il fait bon. (eel fay bohn) It's nice.

Il fait mauvais (eel fay moh-vay) bad

Il fait frais (eel fay fray) cool

Il fait froid (eel fay fwah) cold

Il fait chaud (eel fay shoh) warm, hot

Il fait nuageux (eel fay noo-ah-zhuh) cloudy

Il fait beau (eel fay boh) beautiful

Il fait doux (eel fay dooh) mild

Il fait orageux (eel fay oh-rah-zhuh) stormy

Il fait du soleil (eel fay dew so-lay) sunny

Il fait du vent (eel fay vawn) windy

Il fait du brouillard (eel fay broo-ee-yar) foggy

Il neige (eel nezh) snowing

Il pleut (eel pluh) raining

Il gèle (eel zhell) freezing

16 TIME

France has the second largest rail network in Europe (ninth in the world) making trains the perfect way to tour the country. You don't have to bother with hiring a car, or restrain from a glass of exquisite French wine because you need to drive. With France's high-speed trains everything is taken care of and you are left to enjoy the view while traveling from place to place. But trains are always right on schedule and to catch any of them you need to know the time in French. Besides, how will you be able to comply with the tradition French lunch from 12 PM to 2PM, when almost nothing is open and everyone is enjoying their meals, if you cannot tell the time? You will also want to note that French time is expressed in the 24-hour military format.

Quelle heure est-il? (kell urr ay-teel) What time is it?

Il est... (eel ay) It is...

une heure (oon urr) one o'clock

deux heures (duh zurr) two o'clock

midi (mee-dee) noon

minuit (meen-wee) midnight

trois heures et quart (twa zurr ay car) a quarter after three

une heure precise (oon urr pray-sees) one o'clock sharp

quatre heures précises (ka-truh urr pray-sees) four o'clock sharp

midi et demi (meee-dee ay duh-mee) twelve thirty

six heures et demie (see zurr ay duh-mee) six thirty

sept heures moins le quart (set urr mwahn luh car) a quarter to seven

cinq heures vingt (sank urr vahn) five twenty

onze heures moins dix (ohnz urr mwan dees) ten fifty

du matin (doo mah-tahn) in the morning/AM

de l'après-midi (duh lah-pray mih-dee) in the afternoon/PM

du soir (doo swahr) in the evening/PM

17 FAMILY AND ANIMALS

Studies have shown the French people form very strong bonds with their families and friends. For instance, a survey held in 2013 noted that 93% of the people overviewed felt they had at least one close family member who they could rely on. That same year France proved once again how important family and love are, by legalizing same-sex marriage. But the French people don't only love other humans – they are also enthusiastic about animals. There are about 17 dogs per every 100 people in France which is one of the highest ratios in the world!

la famille (fah-mee) Family

des parents (pahr-awn) Relatives

les grands-parents (grawn-pahr-awn) Grandparents

les parents (pahr-awn) Parents

la mère, maman (mehr, ma-ma) Mom

la belle-mère (bell-mehr) Stepmother/Mother-in-Law

le père, papa (pehr, pa-pa) Dad

le beau-père (boh-pehr) Stepfather/Father-in-Law

la fille (fee) Daughter

le fils (feess) Son

la soeur (sir) Sister

la demi-soeur (duh-mee-sir) Half/Step Sister

la belle-soeur (bell-sir) Sister-in-Law

la belle-fille (bell-fee) Stepdaughter/Daughter-in-Law

le frère (frehr) Brother

le demi-frère (duh-mee-frehr) Half/Step Brother

le beau-frère (boh-frair) Brother-in-Law

le beau-fils (boh-feess) Stepson/Son-in-Law

les jumeaux (zhoo-moh) Twins (m)

les jumelles (zhoo-mell) Twins (f)

l'oncle (ohnk-luh) Uncle

la tante (tawnt) Aunt

la grand-mère (grawn-mehr) Grandmother

le grand-père (grawn-pehr) Grandfather

la cousine (koo-zeen) Cousin (f)

le cousin (koo-zahn) Cousin (m)

la femme (fawn) Wife

le mari (mah-ree) Husband

la femme (fawn) Woman

l'homme (ohm) Man

la fille (fee) Girl

le garçon (gar-sohn) Boy

la nièce (nee-ess) Niece

le neveu (nuh-vuh) Nephew

les petits-enfants (puh-tee-zawn-fawn) Grandchildren

la petite-fille (puh-teet fee) Granddaughter

le petit-fils (puh-tee feez) Grandson

des parents éloignés (pahr-awn zay-lwawn-yay) Distant Relatives

Célibataire (say-lee-bah-tair) Single

marié(e) (mah-ree-ay) Married

séparé(e) (say-pah-ray) Separated

divorcé(e) (dee-vor-say) Divorced

veuf / veuve (vuhf / vuhv) Widower / Widow

Animals

le chien / la chienne (shee-ahn / shee-enn) Dog

le chat / la chatte (shah / shaht) Cat

le chiot (shee-oh) Puppy

le chaton (shah-tohn) Kitten

le cochon (koh-shohn) Pig

le coq (kohk) Rooster

le lapin (lah-pahn) Rabbit

la vache (vahsh) Cow

le cheval (chuh-val) Horse

le canard (kah-nahr) Duck

la chèvre (shev-ruh) Goat

l'oie (lwah) Goose

le mouton (moo-tohn) Sheep

l'agneau (lon-yoh) Lamb

l'âne (lon) Donkey

la souris (soo-ree) Mouse

18 TO KNOW

Did you know the following about France: the popular distress call "Mayday" has been derived from the French "M'aide", meaning "help me"; the glass pyramid above the Louvre museum in Paris is in tribute to the ancient Egyptians and their contributions to the world; stilts may now be used for the purposes of advertising and circus performances, but they were once invented by French shepherds who used them to make their way through wet marshes; both Jim Morrisson and Oscar Wilde spent their final moments in the French capital; Napoleon was in fact 5'6 tall. To know people and facts means to understand France so much better and that is why how you know something is important!

There are two words used to express what you know in French: connaître & savoir. Connaître is used to express that know people or places, and savoir is used to express you know facts. Savoir followed by an infinitive means to know how.

connaître (koh-net-truh) to know people

connais (koh-neh) I know

connais (koh-neh) You know

connaît (koh-neh) He/She knows

connaissons (koh-nezz-ohn) We know

connaissez (koh-nezz-ay) You know

connaissent (koh-nezz) They know

savoir (sahv-wahr) to know facts

sais (say) I know

sais (say) You know

sait (say) He/She knows

savons (sah-vohn) We know

savez (sav-ay) You know

savent (sahv) They know

Je **connais** ton frère. I know your brother.

Je **sais** que ton frère s'appelle Jacques. I know that your brother is named Jack.

Connaissez-vous Paris? Do you know (Are you familiar with) Paris?

Oui, nous **connaissons** Paris. Yes, we know (are familiar with) Paris.

Tu **sais** où Paris se trouve. You know where Paris is located. (Note the difference between *to know of*, and *to know the location* - a fact)

Ils **savent** nager. They know how to swim. (Savoir plus an infinitive means to *know how to do something*)

19 FORMATION OF PLURAL NOUNS

How many paintings are in the Louvre museum? How many floors does the Eiffel Tower have? Do you need just one bean and one tomato for a tradition green bean-tomato salad with herbs? And how will you ever make sausage-stuffed potato galette if you are only able to buy a single potato from the market? Forming plurals in French may not seem quite as straightforward as it is in English, but once you start learning them you will find how simple, and necessary, they actually are!

To make a noun plural, you usually add an -s. But there are some exceptions:

If a noun already ends in an -s, add nothing.

For example,

le bus (bus)

les bu**s** (buses)

If a noun ends in -eu or -eau, add an x.

For example,

le bateau (boat)

les bateau**x** (boats)

If a masculine noun ends in -al or -ail, change it to -aux.

For example,

le cheval (horse)

les chev**aux** (horses)

Some nouns ending in -ou add an -x instead of -s.

For example,

le genou (knee)

les genou**x** (knees)

There are of course some exceptions that you will need to memorize such as un oeil (eye) - des yeux (eyes); as you learn the French language.

20 POSSESSIVE ADJECTIVES

Imagine you have finally gotten your hands on a premium French wine that you have been dreaming of for years, such as the famous Château Rayas, and have decided to share it with some of your new French-speaking friends. You only have a bottle of this wine featuring unique flavors of licorice and lavender, and you have distributed the liquid among the attendees when a friend takes your glasses and drinks it, while you have to stand by silently and watch, without being able to say "This is mine and that one is yours". Learning possessive adjectives in French will certainly help escape awkward situations

My

mon (mohn) masc.

ma (mah) fem.

mes (may) plural

Your

ton (tohn) masc.

ta (tah) fem.

tes (tay) plural

His/Her/Its

son (sohn) masc.

sa (sah) fem.

ses (say) plural

Our

notre (noh-truh) masc.

notre fem.

nos (noh) plural

Your

votre (voh-truh) masc.

votre fem.

vos (voh) plural

Their

leur (luhr) masc.

leur fem.

leurs (luhr) plural

In French, possessive pronouns are placed before the noun. If a feminine noun begins with a vowel, you will need to use the masculine form of the pronoun for ease of pronunciation. For example, ma amie is incorrect and must be changed to mon amie, even though amie is feminine.

C'est ma mère et mon père. *This is my mother and my father.*

Ce sont vos petits-enfants? *These are your grandchildren?*

Mes parents sont divorcés. *My parents are divorced.*

Sa grand-mère est veuve. *His grandmother is a widow.*

Notre frère est marié, mais notre soeur est célibataire. *Our brother is married, but our sister is single.*

Ton oncle est architecte, n'est-ce pas? *Your uncle is an architect, isn't he?*

Leurs cousines sont hollandaises. *Their cousins are Dutch.*

21 TO DO OR MAKE

The French were the ones to make the metric system, the roulette, gothic art, aspirin, antibiotics and chocolate. In fact one of the best things to do in France is visit the historic port of Bayonne, also known as the birthplace of French chocolate. The chocolatiers and the delicious creations made there will amaze you! No wonder the film "Chocolate" was set in a picturesque French city! Another great thing to do in France is experience art and architecture – the diversity and richness is so vast! Just think about the Mona Lisa in the Louvre or Cathédrale St-Etienne de Metz and it's astounding stained glass. Without using to do or to make you will not be able to describe many of the fascinations of France, so don't neglect those essential verbs.

Faire (fair) to do, make

fais (fay) I

fais (fay) You

fait (fay) He/She

faisons (fezz-ohn) We

faites (fett) You

font (fohnt) They do/make

Here are a list of common phrases that utilize faire:

faire le (subject in school) - to do / study (subject)

faire le ménage - to do the housework

faire la cuisine - to do the cooking

faire la lessive - to do laundry

faire la vaisselle - to do the dishes

faire une promenade - to take a walk

faire une voyage - to take a trip

faire les courses - to run errands

faire des achats - to go shopping

faire de l'exercice - to exercise

faire attention - to pay attention

faire la queue - to stand in line

faire de (a sport) - to play (a sport)

faire le sourd / l'innocent - to act deaf / innocent

22 SCHOOL & JOBS

Have you ever considered working or studying in France? Perhaps you would like to wear a barrette as a uniform or be employed in downtown Paris. Even if you don't have such plans, you may find a tour of the world-famous Sorbonne, which nowadays houses the University of Paris, to be quite intriguing. Its gilded ceilings and winded stairs will take your breath away with their beauty and historical importance. Still, to make the best out of it, first you would need to know some basic school and work vocabulary in French.

l'architecte (lar-shee-tekt) architect m.

l'architecte (lar-shee-tekt) architect f.

le comptable (kohn-tahbl) accountant m.

la comptable (kohn-tabl) accountant f.

le juge (zhoozh) judge m.

la juge (zhoozh) judge f.

l'homme d'affaires (lohn dah-fehr) business person m.

la femme d'affaires (fahn dah-fehr) business person f.

le boulanger (boo-lawn-zhay) baker m.

la boulangère (boo-lawn-zhay) baker f.

le coiffeur (kwah-fur) hair dresser m.

la coiffeuse (kwah-fur) f.

le programmeur (proh-grah-mur) computer programmer m.

la programmeuse (proh-grah-mur) computer programmer f.

le secrétaire (suk-ray-tehr) secretary m.

la secrétaire (suk-ray-tehr) secretary f.

l'électricien (ay-lehk-tree-see-ahn) electrician m.

l'électricien (ay-lehk-tree-see-ahn) electrician f.

le mécanicien (may-kah-nee-syahn) mechanic m.

la mécanicienne (may-kah-nee-syenn) mechanic f.

le cuisinier (kwee-zee-nyay) cook m.

la cuisinière (kwee-zee-nyay) f.

le vendeur (vawn-dur) salesperson m.

la vendeuse (vawn-dur) salesperson f.

le pompier (pohn-pyay) fire fighter m.

le pompier (pohn-pyay) fire fighter f.

le plombier (plohn-byay) plumber m.

le plombier (plohn-byay) plumber f.

le bibliothécaire (bee-blee-oh-teh-kehr) librarian m.

la bibliothécaire (bee-blee-oh-teh-kehr) librarian f.

l'agent de police (lah-zhawnd poh-leess) police

officer m.

l'agent de police (lah-zhawnd poh-leess) police officer f.

le journaliste (zhoor-nah-leest) reporter m.

la journaliste (zhoor-nah-leest) reporter f.

l'ouvrier (loov-ree-ay) factory worker m.

l'ouvrière (loov-ree-ay) factory worker f.

le banquier (bahn-kee-ay) banker m.

la banquière (bahn-kee-ay) banker f.

l'avocat (lah-voh-kah) lawyer m.

l'avocate (lah-voh-kah) lawyer f.

le facteur (fah-tur) postal worker m.

la factrice (fah-tur) postal worker f.

le charpentier (shar-pawn-tyay) carpenter m.

le charpentier (shar-pawn-tyay) carpenter f.

l'ingénieur (lahn-zhay-nyur) engineer m.

l'ingénieure (lahn-zhay-nyur) engineer f.

le médecin (mayd-sawn) doctor m.

la médecine (mayd-sawn) doctor f.

l'infirmier (lahn-feer-myay) nurse m.

l'infirmière (lahn-feer-myay) nurse f.

le pharmacien (fahr-mah-see-ahn) pharmacist m.

le pharmacienne (fahr-mah-see-ahn) pharmacist f.

le psychologue (psee-koh-lohg) psychologist m.

la psychologue (psee-koh-lohg) psychologist f.

le dentiste (dawn-teest) dentist m.

la dentiste (dawn-teest) dentist f.

le vétérinaire (vay-tay-ree-nehr) veterinarian m.

la vétérinaire (vay-tay-ree-nehr) veterinarian f.

le chauffeur de taxi (shoh-furd tahk-see) taxi driver m.

le chauffeur de taxi (shoh-furd tahk-see) taxi driver f.

l'écrivain (lay-kree-vahn) writer m.

l'écrivaine (lay-kree-vahn) writer f.

l'instituteur (lahn-stee-tew-tur) teacher m.

l'institutrice (lahn-stee-tew-tur) teacher f.

le professeur (proh-fuh-sur) professor m.

le professeur (proh-fuh-sur) professor.

l'étudiant (lay-tew-dee-awn) student m.

l'étudiante (lay-tew-dee-awnt) student f.

In French you will find that some professions are always masculine, even if the person is a woman.

You will also find that there are words that are always feminine (such as la victime) even if it is referring to a man.

les mathématiques (maht-ee-mah-teek) Math

l'algèbre (lal-zheb) Algebra

le calcul (kahl-kool) Calculus

la géométrie (zhay-oh-may-tree) Geometry

les sciences économiques (see-awns ay-kon-oh-meek) Economics

les langues étrangères (lawn zay-trawn-zhair) Foreign Languages

la linguistique (lahn-gee-steek) Linguistics

la littérature (lee-tay-rah-tur) Literature

la philosophie (fee-loh-soh-fee) Philosophy

la psychologie (p-see-kol-oh-zhee) Psychology

les sciences politiques (see-awns poh-lee-teek) Political Science

l'histoire (f) (ees-twahr) History

la géographie (zhay-oh-grahf-ee) Geography

la physique (fees-eek) Physics

la biologie (bee-ol-oh-zhee) Biology

la chimie (shee-mee) Chemistry

la zoologie (zoh-ol-oh-zhee) Zoology

la botanique (boh-tah-neek) Botany

les arts (zahr) Art

la musique (mew-zeek) Music

la danse (dahns) Dance

le dessin (duh-sahn) Drawing

la peinture (pahn-tur) Painting

l'informatique (ahn-for-mah-teek) Computer Science

la technologie (teck-no-loh-zhee) Technology

l'éducation physique (f) (lay-dew-kah-see-ohn fee-zeek) Physical Education

Unless preceded by an adjective, you will not use the indefinite article before the profession.

Qu'est-ce que vous faites dans la vie? *What do you do for a living?*

Je suis avocate. *I am a lawyer. (fem.)*

Je suis professeur. *I am a professor.*

Je suis étudiant. *I am a student (masc.)*

Où est-ce que vous faites les études? *Where do you study?*

Je vais à l'université de California. *I go to the university of California*

Je fais mes études à l'université de Denver. *I study at the University of Denver.*

Qu'est-ce que vous étudiez? *What do you study?*

Quelles matières étudiez-vous? *What subjects do you study?*

J'étudie les langues étrangères et la linguistique. *I study foreign languages and linguistics.*

Je fais des mathématiques. *I study/do math.*

Ma spécialization est la biologie. *My major is biology.*

23 PREPOSITIONS AND CONTRACTIONS

How would you react if someone asked you what you do on the day? Or if somebody said that they were working onto a publishing company? Prepositions are important in any language – even if you know the vocabulary and verb tenses perfectly, your sentence might not make any sense without the use of the proper prepositions. While prepositions are important for any language, contractions are especially popular with the French speakers. A very unique characteristic of the French language is that it is constantly evolving – words are becoming shorter and easier to learn because of contractions. Getting immersed in this beautiful language is easily done by leaning about prepositions and contractions.

parmi (par-mee) among

à (ah) at / to / in

chez (shay) at the house of

entre (on-truh) between

pour (poohr) for

de (duh) from / of / about

dans (dawn) in

sur (sir) on

avec (ah-veck) with

sans (sawn) without

Forming Contractions

à + le = au (oh) at / to / in the

à + les = aux (oh) at / to / in the (plural)

de + le = du (dew) of / from / about the

de + les = des (day) of / from / about the (pl.)

27. To Come and to Go

Would you like to come with me to Toulouse and see the beautiful old buildings or would your prefer a trip to the world-famous vineyards of Bordeaux? To come and to go are really important to learn in French since mixing them up might lead to the exact opposite result of what you are looking for. Learn how to invite gorgeous French women and dashing French gentlemen to dinner parties with these two invaluable verbs.

Venir (vuh-neer) to come

viens (vee-ahn)

viens (vee-ahn)

vient (vee-ahn)

venons (vuh-nohn)

venez (vuh-nay)

viennent (vee-enn)

Aller (ah-lay) to go

vais (vay)

vas (vah)

va (vah)

allons (ah-lohn)

allez (ah-lay)

vont (vohn)

The verbs tenir - to hold, devenir - to become, obtenir - to get, revenir - to come back are also conjugated like venir.

Je viens des Etats-Unis. *I come from the United States.*

Il tient un crayon. *He's holding a pencil.*

Nous allons en Espagne. *We're going to Spain.*

Tu ne vas pas au Brésil cet été. *You're not going to Brazil this summer.*

Aller + an infinitive signifies "going to do something."

Ils vont aller en Angleterre. *They are going to go to England.*

Elle va parler russe. *She's going to speak Russian.*

Je vais devenir professeur. *I'm going to become a professor.*

Aller is also used when discussing health.

Comment vas-tu? *How are you?*

Je vais bien. *I'm fine.*

Venir de + an infinitive means "to have just done something."

Il vient d'aller à la Finlande. *He just went to Finland.*

Vous venez de manger une pomme. *You just ate an apple.*

24 CONJUGATING REGULAR VERBS

Speak, hear, share, walk, like – verbs you need every day in most conversations. And, of course, since you are learning French you couldn't possibly neglect words such as love and eat – after all, Paris is the ultimate city of love, while the entire country of France offers some of the most intricate meals. Naturally, you would need to use those verbs in more than one conjugation if you would like to have a normal conversation. Don't worry though, they are all regular verbs and you will quickly be able to master the pattern.

In the French language, verbs end in -er, -re, or -ir.

A verb prior to conjugation, is called the infinitive. By removing the last two letters of the verb, you will be left with the stem (for example, aimer is the infinitive, aim- is the stem.)

The present indicative tense indicates an ongoing action, general state, or habitual activity. Besides the simple present tense (I write, I run, I see); there are two other forms of the present tense in English: the progressive (I am writing, I am running, etc.) and the emphatic (I do write, I do run, etc.) However, these three English present tenses are all translated by the present indicative tense in French.

To conjugate verbs in the present tense, use the stem and add the following endings.

-er verbs

-e

-s

-e

-ons

-ez

-ent

aimer -to like, love

j'aim**e** (zhem)

aim**es** (em)

aim**e** (em)

aim**ons** (em-ohn)

aim**ez** (em-ay)

aim**ent** (em)

-re verbs

-s

-s

-

-ons

-ez

-ent

vendre - to sell

vend**s** (vawn)

vend**s** (vawn)

vend (vawn)

vend**ons** (vawn-dohn)

vend**ez** (vawn-day)

vend**ent** (vawn)

1st –ir

-is

-is

-it

-issons

-issez

-issent

finir - to finish

fin**is** (fee-nee)

fin**is** (fee-nee)

fin**it** (fee-nee)

fin**issons** (fee-nee-sohn)

fin**issez** (fee-nee-say)

fin**issent** (fee-neess)

2nd -ir

-s

-s

-t

-ons

-ez

-ent

partir - to leave

par**s** (pahr)

par**s** (pahr)

par**t** (pahr)

part**ons** (pahr-tohn)

part**ez** (pahr-tay)

part**ent** (pahrt)

The 2nd -ir verbs are sometimes considered irregular because there are only a few verbs that follow this pattern. Other verbs like partir are sortir (to go out), dormir (to sleep), mentir (to lie), sentir (to smell, feel) and servir (to serve.)

aimer (em-ay) to like, love

chanter (shahn-tay) to sing

chercher (share-shay) to look for

commencer (koh-mawn-say) to begin

donner (dohn-nay) to give

étudier (ay-too-dee-ay) to study

fermer (fehr-may) to close

habiter (ah-bee-tay) to live

jouer (zhoo-ay) to play

manger (mawn-zhay) to eat

montrer (mohn-tray) to show

parler (par-lay) to speak

penser (pawn-say) to think

travailler (trah-vy-yay) to work

trouver (troo-vay) to find

Regular -re verbs

vendre (vawn-druh) to sell

attendre (ah-tawn-druh) to wait for

entendre (awn-tawn-druh) to listen

perdre (pair-druh) to lose

répondre (à) (ray-pohn-druh ah) to answer

descendre (deh-sawn-druh) to go down

1st –ir verbs

bâtir (bah-teer) to build

finir (fee-neer) to finish

choisir (shwa-zeer) to choose

punir (poo-neer) to punish

remplir (rawn-pleer) to fill

obéir (à) (oh-bay-eer ah) to obey

réussir (ray-oo-seer) to succeed

guérir (gay-reer) to cure, heal

If a verb is followed by à (as is the case with répondre) you have to use the à and any contractions after the conjugated verb.

For example,

Je réponds **au** téléphone.

25 TO TAKE, EAT OR DRINK

Since a large part of the French culture is connected to food and drink, you can only improve your French experience by learning verbs such as to take, eat or drink. To eat on a picnic blanket in the midst of a road trip or to drink Loire Valley wine is to take in French culture! With the abundance of fine wine and food that France has to offer, you would simply need those verbs to be able to tell the stories of your great experiences.

Prendre (prawn-druh) to take, eat or drink

prends (prawn)

prends (prawn)

prend (prawn)

prenons (pruh-nohn)

prenez (pru-nay)

prennent (prenn)

Other French verbs that are conjugated like prendre: apprendre - to learn, comprendre - to understand and surprendre - to surprise.

Boire (bwahr) to drink

bois (bwah)

bois (bwah)

boit (bwah)

buvons (bew-vohn)

buvez (bew-vay)

boivent (bwahv)

If you would like to say "I am having wine," the French translation is "Je prends **du** vin." It is important to use de and le, la, l', or les and the proper contractions (called partitives) because in French you must also express some. For example, "je prends **de la** bière" literally means "I am having some beer" even though in English we would usually only say I am having beer.

Manger is a regular verb that means "to eat," however manger is used in a general sense.

For example,

Je **mange** le poulet tous les samedis. *I eat chicken every Saturday.*

Boire is literally the verb to drink and is also used in a general sense only.

For example,

Je bois du vin tout le temps (*I drink wine all the time*) instead of Je prends du vin (I am having wine)

26 FOOD AND MEALS

A survey done in 2013 has shown that the average French eats about 500 snails each year. If this does not sound too appealing to you, then you probably have not yet tried the famous French snails prepared with garlic and herb butter. Of course not every French person enjoys snails, but there is a lot more to choose from – after all this is the country with some of the most iconic culinary masterpieces. French food tends to be very delicate and balanced, a blend of luxury and taste. After all, gourmet food stems from the French kitchens, the word's translation from French is "a connoisseur of fine food and drink". On your next trip to France, make sure to try some of their most famous meals such as the onion soup, beef bourguignon, Salade nicoise made with fresh vegetables, eggs and tuna, as well as the mouth-watering vegetable Ratatouille dish. And of course, who could forget about French cheese or divine chocolate soufflés? The food is an exceptional part of France, no wonder many culinary excursions are being organized throughout the year. Of course with such amazing food the French cannot help but pay special attention to their meals. Even a picnic on a blanket at the park can turn into a gourmet affair! Learn the words for foods and meals in French and come a little closer to this amazing cuisine!

le petit déjeuner (puh-tee day-zhew-nay) Breakfast

le déjeuner (day-zhew-nay) Lunch

le dîner (dee-nay) Dinner

la tasse (tahss) Cup

la tranche (trawnsh) Slice

le bol (bohl) Bowl

le verre (verr) Glass

le sel et le poivre (luh sell ay luh pwahv-ruh) Salt and Pepper

la fourchette (foor-shett) Fork

la cuillère (kwee-yehr) Spoon

le couteau (koo-toh) Knife

l'assiette (f) (ah-syett) Plate

la serviette (ser-vyett) Napkin

la glace (glahss) Ice cream

le jus (zhew) Juice

le fruit (fwee) Fruit

le fromage (froh-mawzh) Cheese

le poulet (poo-lay) Chicken

l'oeuf (m) (luff) Egg

le gâteau (gah-toh) Cake

la tarte (tart) Pie

le lait (leh) Milk

le café (kah-fay) Coffee

le beurre (burr) Butter

l'eau (loh) Water

le jambon (zham-bohn) Ham

le poisson (pwah-sohn) Fish

le thé (tay) Tea

la salade (sah-lahd) Salad

la confiture (kon-fee-chur) Jam

la viande (vee-awnd) Meat

les frites (f) (freet) French fries

la bière (bee-ehr) Beer

le vin (vahn) Wine

le sucre (soo-kruh) Sugar

le potage (poh-tawzh) Soup

27 FRUITS, VEGETABLES, MEATS

As you already know, the French have a real appreciation for food and so it is always important for quality fruits, vegetables and meats to go into their dishes. If you are ever in Paris, twice a week you can become part of the event that is the Marché Bastille food market. Only the freshest, most delicious ingredients can be found there, but how would you buy them if you don't know the names for them?

Not only do the French care about good food, but they also place a huge importance on the global problem that is wasting it. In 2014 a supermarket chain organized a clever campaign called "Inglorious fruits & vegetables" where they sold misshapen, but otherwise fine produce at 30% off to stimulate better utilization of food products. Support this great French cause by learning the words for fruits, vegetables and meats!

un fruit (fwee) fruit

le maïs (mah-eez) corn

une pomme (pohm) apple

un concombre (cohn-cohn-bruh) cucumber

un abricot (ah-bree-koh) apricot

une aubergine (oh-behr-zheen) eggplant

une banane (bah-nahn) banana

la laitue (leh-tew) lettuce

une myrtille (meer-tee) blueberry

un champignon (shahm-pee-nyohn) mushroom

une cerise (suh-reez) cherry

un oignon (wawn-yohn) onion

une noix de coco (nwah duh koh-koh) coconut

les pois (pwah) peas

une date (daht) date

un piment (pee-mawn) pepper

une figue (feeg) fig

une pomme de terre (pohm duh tehr) potato

un raisin (reh-zahn) grape

une citrouille (see-troo-ee) pumpkin

un pamplemousse (pahm-pluh-moos) grapefruit

le riz (reez) rice

un citron (see-trohn) lemon

des épinards (ay-pee-nar) spinach

un limon (lee-mohn) lime

une courge (koorzh) squash

un melon (mel-ohn) melon

une tomate (to-maht) tomato

une olive (oh-leev) olive

un navet (nah-vay) turnip

une orange (oh-ranzh) orange

des courgettes (koor-zhett) zucchini

une pêche (pesh) peach

une viande (vee-awnd) meat

une poire (pwahr) pear

du lard, du bacon (lar, bah-kohn) bacon

un ananas (ah-nah-nah) pineapple

le bifteck (beef-teck) beef

une prune (prewn) plum

un poulet (poo-lay) chicken

un pruneau (proo-noh) prune

un canard (kah-nar) duck

un raisin sec (reh-zahn sek) raisin

une chèvre (shev-ruh) goat

une framboise (frwahm-bwahz) raspberry

le jambon (zhahm-bohn) ham

une fraise (frez) strawberry

l'agneau (awn-yoh) lamb

une pastèque (pah-stek) watermelon

le foie (fwah) liver

une legume (leh-goom) vegetable

des boulettes de viande (boo-lett duh vee-awnd) meatballs

un artichaut (ar-tee-sho) artichoke

une côtelette de porc (kote-lett duh pork) pork chop

des asperges (ahs-pehrzh) asparagus

un lapin (lah-pahn) rabbit

une betterave (bett-rahv) beet

une côte de boeuf (kote duh buf) T-bone steak

le broccoli (broh-coh-lee) broccoli

la saucisse (so-seess) sausage

un chou (shoo) cabbage

une dinde (dahnd) turkey

une carotte (cah-roht) carrot

le veau (voh) veal

un chou-fleur (shoo-flir) cauliflower

un chevreuil (shuv-ruh-ee) venison

un céléri (say-lay-ree) celery

28 QUANTITIES

France produces around 400 kinds of cheese, 7-8 billion bottles of wine per year and the Grand Extrait edition of the Chanel #5 perfume is 30 ounces a bottle. Quantities matter whether you are visiting a food maker, a winery, a fashion store or simply want to learn a bit about French statistics. Learning how to express a desired quantity in French is invaluable even if you are just dabbling into the culture and would like to start by preparing a French meal right at home.

assez de enough (of)

un morceau de *a piece of*

une douzaine de *a dozen of*

une assiette de *a plate of*

un peu de *a little (bit) of*

un paquet de *a packet of*

beaucoup de *a lot of*

une tasse de *a cup of*

un panier de *a basket of*

une boîte de *a box of*

une tranche de *a slice of*

une poignée de *a handful of*

une bouteille de *a bottle of*

trop de *too much, many*

plus de *more*

un kilo de *a kilo of*

un verre de *a glass of*

un bouquet de *a bunch of*

Je voudrais un morceau de tarte. *I would like one piece of pie.*

Je voudrais prendre du fromage, mais pas de fruit. *I would like to have some cheese, but no fruit.*

Est-ce que je peux prendre un verre de vin? *May I have a glass of wine?*

Il prend de la viande. *He is eating some meat.*

Nous prenons du riz et du brocoli. *We are having some rice and broccoli.*

Je prends du vin. *I'm drinking some wine.*

Je ne prends pas de vin. *I am not drinking any wine.*

Il y a trop de lait dans la tasse. *There is too much milk in the cup.*

29 IRREGULARITIES IN REGULAR VERBS

In the French Alps you can have a fantastic ski vacation during the winter, at resorts such as the Chamonix region, or take long, breath-taking hikes during the summer and stop for a baguette and cheese picnic. However, be careful what car you choose to get there as some of the roads curve extensively, just like some French grammar rules – even the regular verbs have some natural irregularities. Here you can learn what they are.

Verbs that end in -cer and -ger: Did you know that the nous form of manger isn't mangons, but mangeons? Why? The e has to remain so the g can keep its soft sound. Additionally, the nous form of commencer isn't commencons, but commençons. In this instance, the c must have the accent (called a cedilla) under it to retain the c sound soft.

manger-to eat

mange (mawnzh)

manges (mawnzh)

mange (mawnzh)

mangeons (mawn-zhohn)

mangez (mawn-zhay)

mangent (mawnzh)

commencer-to begin

commence (koh-mawnz)

commences (koh-mawnz)

commence (koh-mawnz)

commençons (koh-mawn-sohn)

commencez (koh-mawn-say)

commencent (koh-mawnz)

The accent grave: There are some verbs in French that add or change to an accent grave **(è)** in all the forms except the nous and vous.

espérer-to hope

j'esp**è**re (zhess-pehr)

esp**è**res (ess-pehr)

esp**è**re (ess-pehr)

esp**é**rons (ess-pay-rohn)

esp**é**rez (ess-pay-ray)

esp**è**rent (ess-pehr)

acheter-to buy

j'ach**è**te (zhah-shet)

ach**è**tes (ah-shet)

achète (ah-shet)

achetons (ahsh-tohn)

achetez (ahsh-tay)

achètent (ah-shet)

The verbs that are conjugated as -er verbs: You will find in French that some **-ir verbs** are conjugated like **-er verbs**.

offrir-to offer

j'offr**e** (zhaw-fruh)

offr**es** (aw-fruh)

offr**e** (aw-fruh)

offr**ons** (aw-frohn)

offr**ez** (aw-fray)

offr**ent** (aw-fruh)

Verbs that are conjugated in this manner, like offrir, include: découvrir-to discover, couvrir-to cover, ouvrir-to open and souffrir-to suffer.

Verbs that end in -yer: With verbs that end in yer, change the y to an i in every form except the nous and vous.

envoyer-to send

j'envo**ie** (zhawn-vwah)

envo**ies** (awn-vwah)

envo**ie** (awn-vwah)

envo**yons** (awn-vwah-yohn)

envo**yez** (awn-vwah-yay)

envo**ient** (awn-vwah)

Other verbs conjugated in the same manner as envoyer (awn-vwah-yay) include:

essayer (ess-ah-yay) to try

nettoyer (nuh-twah-yay) to clean

Verbs that double the consonant: Verbs, such as jeter-to throw (zheh-tay) and appeler-to call (ahp-lay) double the consonant in all forms except the nous and vous.

appeler-to call

j'appe**lle** (zhah-pell)

appe**lles** (ah-pell)

appe**lle** (ah-pell)

appelons (ahp-lohn)

appelez (ahp-lay)

appe**llant** (ah-pell)

30 PAST INDEFINITE TENSE

Imagine you have gone on a trip to France and met some great people there who have become your friends, but then had to go back home. You and your French friends have decided to keep in touch online but they don't speak English and whenever you try to describe your day they get confused because you don't know how to use the Past Indefinite Tense. Learn how to describe your past experiences with this lesson!

If you want to say something happened, or has happened in French, you have to use the passé composé. It's actually quite simple once you get the hang of it because all you need to learn are the past participles of the verbs.

Regular Verbs: Formation of the Past Participle

-er verbs: é

-re verbs: u

-ir verbs: i

To create a sentence in the past tense, simply conjugate avoir and add the correct past participle based on the verb ending.

For example,

Tu **as habité** ici? *You lived here?* (habiter)

J'ai aimé le concert. *I liked the concert.* (aimer)

Il **a répondu** au téléphone. *He answered the*

telephone. (responder)

Nous **avons fini** le projet. We finished the project. (finir)

To make the past tense negative, add the ne and pas around the conjugated form of avoir.

For example,

Je **n**'ai **pas** aimé le concert. *I didn't like the concert.*

Il **n**'a **pas** répondu. *He didn't answer.*

31 IRREGULAR PAST PARTICIPLES

Some pretty strange and funny things have happened in the past of French history. For instance, you probably didn't know that April Fool's Day dates back to 16th century France. King Charles XIV, who was on the throne at the time, decided to change the calendar. Consequently those who still celebrated New Year's Eve on the 1st of April, as was the old tradition, were ridiculed. Nowadays it is a tradition among French children to stick paper fish on each other's backs with the expression "April Fish". Some strange things also happen in grammar, but you will easily grasp them with this lesson on Irregular Past Participles.

Here is a cheat sheet of irregualar past participles. As with regular verbs, which you learned in the last chapter, to create a sentence in the past tense, conjugate avoir and add the correct past participle.

avoir *to have*: eu (ew) *had*

ouvrir *to open*: ouvert (oo-vehr) opened

connaître *to know*: connu *known*

offrir *to offer*: offert *offered*

croire *to believe*: cru *believed*

pouvoir *to be able to*: pu *was able to*

devoir *to have to*: dû *had to*

prendre *to take*: pris (pree) *taken*

dire *to tell*: dit *said*

apprendre *to learn*: appris *learned*

écrire *to write*: écrit *written*

comprendre *to understand*: compris *understood*

être *to be*: été *been*

surprendre *to surprise*: surprise *surprised*

faire *to do, make*: fait *made*

recevoir *to receive*: reçu (reh-sew) *received*

lire *to read*: lu *read*

rire *to laugh*: ri *laughed*

mettre *to put*: mis (me) *put*

savoir *to know*: su *known*

permettre to *permit*: permis *permitted*

voir *to see*: vu *seen*

promettre *to promise*: promis *promised*

vouloir *to want*: voulu (voo-lew) *wanted*

32 ETRE VERBS

The French, especially in large cities such as Paris and Marseille, may seem a little distant at first glance, but they actually live in very tight-knit communities and love helping each other. Even if you have chosen a large city as your next French destination, you will find that it is easy to ask people for help with directions or a wine and meal recommendation at a nice restaurant. Logically enough, French grammar seems to follow the spirit of its people and has some verbs called helping verbs or auxiliary verbs. Etre is such a verb but it is important to remember that not all other verbs can be combined with etre. This lesson will help you remember the etre verbs so that you can use them to offer and ask for help in French, as well as say many other things.

There are sixteen "house" verbs that are conjugated with être, and they must agree in gender and number with the subject.

The sixteen house verbs are:

aller-*to go*

sortir-*to go out*

venir-*to come*

mourir-*to die*

arriver-*to arrive*

partir-*to leave*

devenir-*to become*

monter-*to go up*

entrer-*to enter*

tomber-*to fall*

revenir-*to come back*

rester-*to stay*

rentrer-*to return home*

naître-*to be born*

passer-*to go by (pass)*

descendre-*to go down*

With an être verb, you will need to use the appropriate form of être followed by the conjugated verb.

Here is an example using the être verb **rester** (to stay),

Je **suis resté**(e)

Tu **es resté**(e)

Il **est resté**

Elle **est restée**

Nous **sommes resté(e)s**

Vous **êtes resté(e)(s)**

Ils **sont restés**

Elles **sont restées**

Don't forget to add the e for feminine and s for plural. Vous can have either of these endings.

33 HOLIDAY PHRASES

The French participate in common festivities such as Easter, Christmas and New Year, but they also have some more specific holidays. For instance, on the 1st of May is the Work Holiday when all workers get a paid day off and trade unions traditionally protest in large cities. It is also Lilly-of-the-valley-day and it is customary for people to exchange the flower. On the 14th of July is another very interesting holiday – Bastille Day, commemorating the storming of the Bastille on the same day in 1789. Throughout the country there are fireworks and traditional dancing parties, while in Paris a military parade passes along the Champs Elysees. Learning the holiday phrases in French will help you immerse yourself in this culture of traditional festive fun.

Joyeux Noël (zhoy-uh no-ell) *Merry Christmas*

Bonne Année (bun ah-nay) *Happy New Year*

Bonne Action de graces (bun ak-see-ohn de grahss) *Happy Thanksgiving*

Joyeuses Pâques (zhoy-uhss pawk) *Happy Easter*

Bonne Halloween (bun ah-loh-ween) *Happy Halloween*

Bonne Saint-Valentin (bun sahnt-val-awn-than) *Happy Valentine's Day*

Bon Anniversaire (bohn ahn-nee-vair-sair) *Happy Birthday*

Printed in Great Britain
by Amazon